the east-west house

noguchi's childhood in japan

christy hale

DISCARDED

Lee & Low Books Inc.
New York

To my brother-in-law, Jeff Apostolou

The following pronunciations are adapted from Japanese for spoken English.
Some variations may exist.

akari *(ah-kah-ree)*   Isamu *(ee-sah-moo)*

Chigasaki *(chee-gah-sah-kee)*   Noguchi *(noh-goo-chee)*

Fuji *(foo-jee)*   shoji *(shoh-jee)*

gaijin *(gah-ee-jeen)*   Yonejiro *(yoh-neh-jee-roh)*

ACKNOWLEDGMENTS

Thanks to Karin Higa, curator at the Japanese American National Museum; and to Amy Hau, administrative director, and Heidi B. Coleman, photo archivist, at The Noguchi Museum, for their assistance in research. Thanks to David and Sachiko Hale for their help translating Japanese. And thanks to Philip Lee, Louise May, Amy Novesky, the Stanford Writing class, and my critique groups for their guidance and encouragement.

———————————

1 2 3 4 5 6 7 8 9 10   First Edition

Library of Congress Cataloging-in-Publication Data   Hale, Christy. The East-West house : Noguchi's childhood in Japan / Christy Hale. — 1st ed.   p. cm.   Summary: "A biography of Isamu Noguchi, Japanese American artist, sculptor, and landscape architect, focusing on his boyhood in Japan, his mixed heritage, and his participation in designing and building a home that fused Eastern and Western influences. Includes an afterword about Noguchi's adult life and works, plus photographs"—Provided by publisher. ISBN 978-1-60060-363-1 (hardcover : alk. paper) 1. Noguchi, Isamu, 1904-1988—Childhood and youth—Juvenile literature. 2. Japanese American sculptors—Biography—Juvenile literature. I. Title.   NB237.N6H35   2009   709.2—dc22   [B]   2008053728

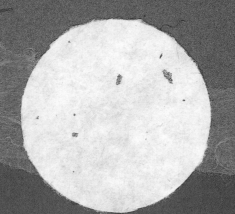

In 1901, Japanese poet Yonejiro Noguchi arrived in New York. Although he had already published two books of poetry in English, Yone was still unsure of the language. He advertised for assistance and hired Leonie Gilmour, a Scotch-Irish American editor and teacher. The two worked well together, and soon a romance developed. Yone declared his love for Leonie and promised they would marry. But in the spring of 1904, Yone suddenly returned to Japan even though Leonie was expecting their child. Leonie and her mother then moved to Los Angeles, where the baby was born on November 17, 1904.

Yone realized he still needed Leonie's help with his English works, and he tried to convince her to come to Japan. Leonie refused at first but finally decided to go. She feared that growing anti-Japanese sentiment in the United States would affect her biracial child. So in March 1907, Leonie and her two-year-old son journeyed from the West to the East.

father's house in Tokyo glowed
with moonlight through *shoji* screens.
Shadows on the wall moved like waves
as tiny fingers curled in play.

With Mama he had sailed countless days
from America to this unknown place.
Then a stranger-father chose his name:
Isamu, Mr. Courageous.

Now father had another family.
His home was not their harbor.
Outside, a bamboo flute cried through barren trees
and a chilly wind scattered leaves.

Unwelcome, yet they remained—
never long in any place.
They were *gaijin*, foreigners,
shunned by everyone.

Together they explored Japan,
sat silently in gardens.
Isamu listened to wind and current.
He held each leaf up close.

He walked watching shadows shift.
Light on stone revealed secret colors.
Water mirrored shapes above—
a kaleidoscope in motion.

Earth, rock, flowers, trees—
these were Isamu's trusted friends.
He dug deep to make his own stream
and steered its course with a stone.

At school he tried to join in play
but others teased and turned from him.
Left out and alone, Isamu made
a different kind of joy.

He molded clay to form a wave,
then painted it blue like Mama's eyes.
Holding soft earth in his hands
he almost forgot his loneliness.

Mama bought a tiny wedge of land
under Chigasaki pines.
An unwanted, awkward, sloping lot
looking out to sea.

Only eight, Isamu drew up plans
to make a small, distinctive house.
Half Eastern, half Western in design,
it was a mixture like his own.

He supervised construction,
watched each detail with care.
Evenings he shared his notes with Mama—
reports of his dreams growing tall.

Three rooms laid out on the bottom floor
and one large room on top.
The builders done, now it remained
for Isamu to add his touch.

Apprenticed to a carpenter,
he sculpted waves in cherry wood.
Carved panels for the sliding doors
that moved from east to west, and back again.

He nestled close to Mama's side
as she read him myths of ancient Greece.
Outside their window Mount Fuji swelled—
inspiration for Isamu to hold.

With the world in his hands
his imagination soared.
And where emptiness once lived,
Isamu created home.

Isamu at age six, 1910

"My longing for affiliation has been the source of my creativity."

—Isamu Noguchi

Isamu Noguchi, 1951

isamu and his mother arrived in Yokohama, Japan, on March 26, 1907, after a seventeen-day crossing of the Pacific Ocean aboard the steamship *Mongolia*. Yonejiro Noguchi met them, and they traveled to his home in Tokyo. Yone's relationship with Leonie was strained, and he was often away. Eventually Leonie became aware that Yone had married a Japanese woman and was keeping two households. Leonie and Isamu moved out of Yone's house, but remained in Japan. Yone had no further presence in Isamu's boyhood.

Yonejiro Noguchi, 1904   *Leonie Gilmour, 1912*

His father's abandonment and his own mixed racial and cultural heritage were constant sources of confusion and discomfort for Isamu. His hair was wavy, and he wore Western-style clothing—so different from the Japanese children, who bullied him regularly. "Whatever situation I was in, I felt not quite one of them," Noguchi later said of his early social world.

Leonie Gilmour provided education, inspiration, and direction in young Isamu's life. She witnessed the prejudice he experienced as a biracial child. She also noted his pleasure and skill in creating with his hands. Leonie steered Isamu toward the arts as a way of blending the conflicting parts of his life, and gave him an opportunity to incorporate both parts of his heritage into the house they built in Chigasaki. The architecture mixed Western-style floorboards and windows with Japanese-style rooms with sliding doors. Isamu closely monitored the carpenters' work. During his later apprenticeship with a local cabinetmaker, Isamu learned to use Japanese tools and added his own carvings and constructions to the Chigasaki house. Leonie taught Isamu botany, and he created his own garden for their home.

Childhood ended abruptly for Isamu in 1918. At age thirteen his mother sent him to Interlaken, an innovative boarding school in Indiana where boys could work with their hands in a shop or in the garden. The school closed shortly after

The "East-West" house, Chigasaki, Japan

Isamu arrived and became an army training camp for World War I. Dr. Edward Rumely, the school's founder, arranged for Isamu to attend a local high school. After graduation, Isamu wanted to become an artist, but Rumely guided him to study medicine, a more stable profession, at Columbia University in New York City.

Leonie moved to New York in 1924 and encouraged her son to enroll in an evening sculpture class at the Leonardo da Vinci Art School. Three months later Isamu had his first exhibit, and his career as a sculptor was launched. He dropped out of medical school to pursue art full-time. Isamu then changed his last name from Gilmour to Noguchi, which signified a feeling of reconnection with his artistic roots in Japan.

Several mentors played significant roles in Isamu Noguchi's creative journey. His first teacher, Onorio Ruotolo at the da Vinci school, taught him traditional sculpture techniques. In Paris in 1928, as an assistant to sculptor Constantin Brancusi, Noguchi learned to use his tools to work directly on the materials he was sculpting; to simplify line and form; and to explore less realistic, more abstract ways of expression.

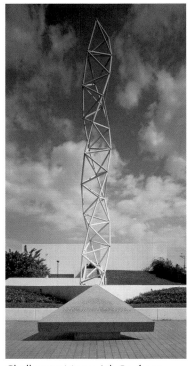

Challenger Memorial, *Bayfront Park, Miami, Florida, 1987*

Globular, *early abstract sculpture, 1928*

Appalachian Spring *stage set for Martha Graham, 1944*

Strange Bird *(aluminum), 1971*

Back in New York in 1929, Noguchi supported himself by making busts of wealthy and famous people. One of the people he met was choreographer Martha Graham. He later collaborated with her for more than thirty years, designing theater sets that allowed dancers and objects to move freely through space.

Noguchi came to think of sculpture as more than just static, three-dimensional objects. His sculptures expressed movement. They presented different views and changing patterns of light and shadow, and gave space a sense of depth. His imaginative garden and playground designs encouraged people's active participation.

R. Buckminster Fuller, the architect, inventor, and visionary, became an intellectual influence on Noguchi, as well as a lifelong friend. The two explored how people live in their environments, and together they planned projects and made models of their ideas.

Slide Mantra, *Odori Park, Sapporo, Japan, 1988–1990*

Mure studio yard with sculptures, Shikoku, Japan

The Noguchi Museum garden, Long Island City, New York

Noguchi with Small Practices, *1979*

Akari lamp, 1963

The influences on Noguchi were many, but his love of earth, craftsmanship, and tools began in Japan. The airy, rice paper *akari* lamps he created were inspired by his earliest memories of moonlight shining through *shoji* screens in his father's home. Japanese gardens, which represent nature artistically for everyday enjoyment, shaped his desire "to bring sculpture into a more direct involvement with the common experience of living," Noguchi said. For more than six decades he worked toward this goal, bringing together ancient and modern, craft and technology, East and West.

Before he died on December 30, 1988, at the age of eighty-four, Isamu Noguchi created two places to showcase his work: The Noguchi Museum in New York and the studio complex in Mure on the Japanese island of Shikoku. At these locations and others around the world, Noguchi's sculptures, furniture, and public spaces live on, dynamic testaments to the creative achievements of one of the twentieth century's most innovative artists.

PHOTOGRAPH CREDITS

The Noguchi Museum: Isamu on bicycle in Chigasaki; Yonejiro Noguchi; Leonie Gilmour; house at Chigasaki, photo by Isamu Noguchi, ©1950–1952. Ken Domon Museum of Photography: Isamu Noguchi, photo by Ken Domon. ©2009 The Isamu Noguchi Foundation and Garden Museum, New York/Artists Rights Society (ARS), New York: *Globular* and *Strange Bird (Unknown Bird)*, photos by Kevin Noble; *Appalachian Spring*; *Slide Mantra* and *Small Practices*, photos by Michio Noguchi; Sculpture Garden, The Noguchi Museum, photo by Elizabeth Felicella; Akari lamp model 55D. Kozo Watabiki: *Challenger Memorial* and yard at Mure studio, photos by Kozo Watabiki. All photographs courtesy of The Noguchi Museum, New York.

QUOTATION SOURCES

p. 30: "My longing . . . my creativity." Duus, Masayo. *The Life of Isamu Noguchi: Journey Without Borders*, from *Ōsaka mainichi*, November 20, 1984.
"Whatever situation . . . of them." Ibid., Noguchi tape transcript.
p. 32: "to bring . . . of living." Noguchi, Isamu. *Isamu Noguchi: A Sculptor's World.*

SOURCES

Altshuler, Bruce. *Isamu Noguchi*. New York: Abbeville Press, 1994.

Ashton, Dore. *Noguchi East and West*. New York: Alfred A. Knopf, 1992.

Duus, Masayo. *The Life of Isamu Noguchi: Journey Without Borders*. Princeton, NJ: Princeton University Press, 2004.

Hunter, Sam. *Isamu Noguchi*. New York: Abbeville Press, 1978.

Isamu Noguchi: Stones and Paper. VHS. Directed by Hiro Narita. New York: Pictures & Words, in association with Thirteen-WNET, 1997.

Kuh, Katherine. "An Interview with Isamu Noguchi." *Horizon*, March 11, 1960: 104–112.

Noguchi, Isamu. *Isamu Noguchi: A Sculptor's World*. Foreword by R. Buckminster Fuller. New York: Harper & Row, 1968.

———. *Isamu Noguchi: Essays and Conversations*. Edited by Diane Apostolos-Cappadona and Bruce Altshuler. New York: Harry N. Abrams, in association with the Isamu Noguchi Foundation, 1994.

———. *Isamu Noguchi: Space of Akari & Stone*. San Francisco: Chronicle Books, 1985.

Noguchi, Yone. "Isamu's Arrival in Japan." *Nation*, February 11, 1911: 798–800.

Portrait of an Artist: Isamu Noguchi. VHS. Directed by Charlotte Mitchell Zwerin. New York: Whitgate Productions, 1980.

Tobias, Tobi. *Isamu Noguchi: The Life of a Sculptor*. New York: Thomas Y. Crowell/HarperCollins, 1974.